PRO HOCKEY'S

UNDERDOGS:

PLAYERS AND TEAMS WHO SHOCKED THE HOCKEY WORLD

BY MICHAEL BRADLEY

CAPSTONE PRESS
a capstone imprint

Sports Illustrated Kids Sports Shockers! are published by Capstone Press,
1710 Roe Crest Drive, North Mankato, Minnesota 56003
www.mycapstone.com

Library of Congress Cataloging-in-Publication data
Names: Bradley, Michael, 1962- author.
Title: Pro Hockey's Underdogs : Players and Teams Who Shocked the Hockey World /
by Michael Bradley.
Description: North Mankato, Minnesota : Capstone Press, 2017. | Series: Sports
Illustrated Kids. Sports Shockers!
Identifiers: LCCN 2017004670| ISBN 9781515780458 (library binding) | ISBN
9781515780496 (eBook PDF) Subjects: LCSH: Hockey—United States—History—
Juvenile literature. | Hockey players—United States—Biography—Juvenile literature.
| Hockey—Canada—History—Juvenile literature. | Hockey players—Canada—
Biography—Juvenile literature.
Classification: LCC GV847.25 B75 2017 | DDC 796.962/64—dc23
LC record available at https://lccn.loc.gov/2017004670

Editorial Credits
Nick Healy, editor; Kyle Grenz, designer; Eric Gohl, media researcher;
Kathy McColley, production specialist

Photo Credits
AP Photo: 10–11, Richard Sheinwald, 25; Getty Images: Bruce Bennett, 4, 18, 19 (top),
24, Sports Illustrated/George Tiedemann, 19 (bottom); Newscom: Cal Sport Media/
Nick Wagner, 26, 27, Reuters/Mike Blake, 6; Shutterstock: Eugene Onischenko, cover
(left), Vanessa Belfiore, cover (right); Sports Illustrated: Damian Strohmeyer, 16, 17,
20, 21, David E. Klutho, 7, 8, 9, 14, 15, 22, 23, 30, 31 (bottom), Heinz Kluetmeier, 28, 29,
John D. Hanlon, 12, 13, Lane Stewart, 5, Simon Bruty, 31 (top)

Printed and bound in the USA.
010364F17

Table of Contents

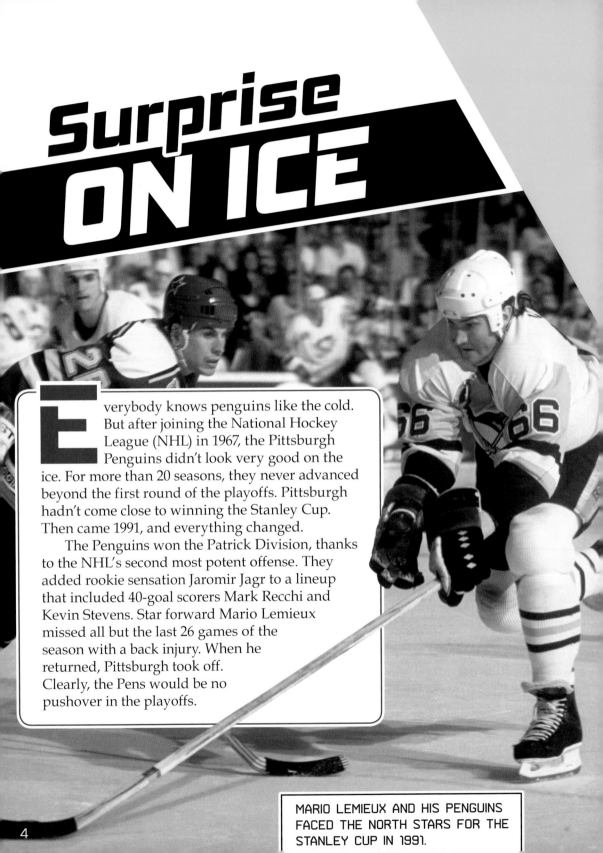

Surprise
ON ICE

Everybody knows penguins like the cold. But after joining the National Hockey League (NHL) in 1967, the Pittsburgh Penguins didn't look very good on the ice. For more than 20 seasons, they never advanced beyond the first round of the playoffs. Pittsburgh hadn't come close to winning the Stanley Cup. Then came 1991, and everything changed.

The Penguins won the Patrick Division, thanks to the NHL's second most potent offense. They added rookie sensation Jaromir Jagr to a lineup that included 40-goal scorers Mark Recchi and Kevin Stevens. Star forward Mario Lemieux missed all but the last 26 games of the season with a back injury. When he returned, Pittsburgh took off. Clearly, the Pens would be no pushover in the playoffs.

MARIO LEMIEUX AND HIS PENGUINS FACED THE NORTH STARS FOR THE STANLEY CUP IN 1991.

The Penguins needed seven games to overcome the New Jersey Devils in the first round. Pittsburgh reached uncharted waters by whipping the Washington Capitals four games to one in the division finals. Up next were the Boston Bruins, who had collected the most points in the Wales Conference.

Pittsburgh spotted the Bruins two wins and then ripped off four straight victories to reach the Stanley Cup Finals. The Penguins were breaking new ground, but their opponent was an even bigger surprise. Minnesota's North Stars, who had managed just 68 points and finished seventh in the Campbell Conference, had somehow beaten three heavyweights to reach the final round.

WAS PITTSBURGH'S MAGICAL SEASON GOING TO BE SPOILED BY THE ULTIMATE CINDERELLA? COULD THE PENGUINS JOIN OTHER HOCKEY UNDERDOGS AND BREAK THROUGH THE ICE?

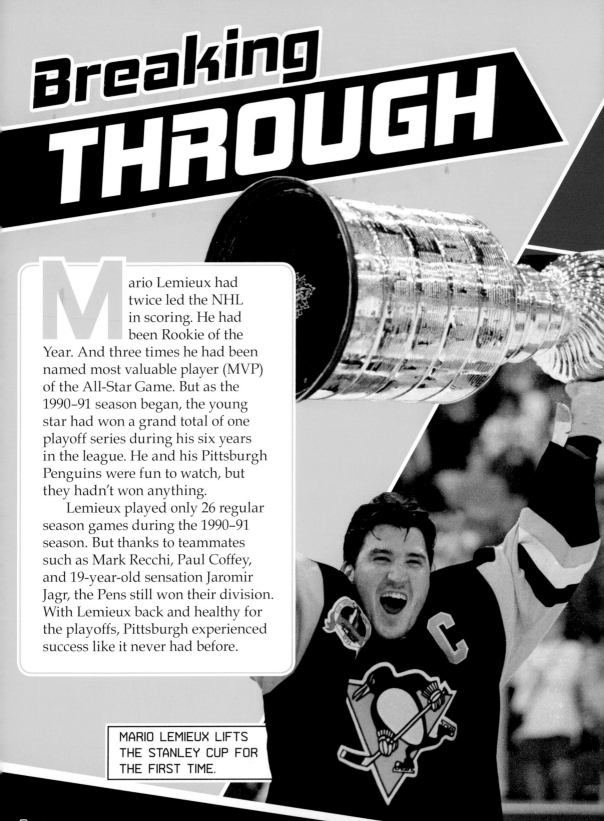

Breaking THROUGH

Mario Lemieux had twice led the NHL in scoring. He had been Rookie of the Year. And three times he had been named most valuable player (MVP) of the All-Star Game. But as the 1990–91 season began, the young star had won a grand total of one playoff series during his six years in the league. He and his Pittsburgh Penguins were fun to watch, but they hadn't won anything.

Lemieux played only 26 regular season games during the 1990–91 season. But thanks to teammates such as Mark Recchi, Paul Coffey, and 19-year-old sensation Jaromir Jagr, the Pens still won their division. With Lemieux back and healthy for the playoffs, Pittsburgh experienced success like it never had before.

MARIO LEMIEUX LIFTS THE STANLEY CUP FOR THE FIRST TIME.

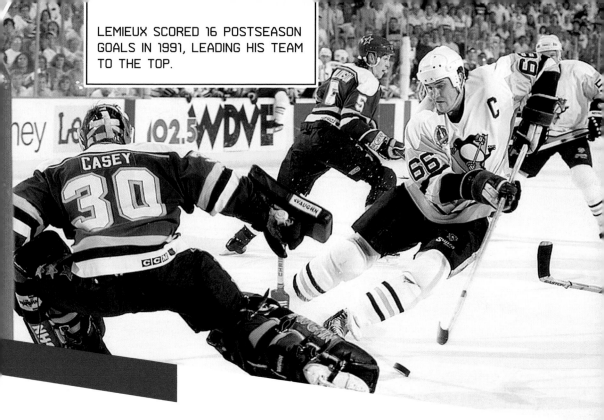

LEMIEUX SCORED 16 POSTSEASON GOALS IN 1991, LEADING HIS TEAM TO THE TOP.

Despite winning their division, the Penguins had the third-best record in their conference. Boston had 12 more points in the regular season and were expected to win the conference. Pittsburgh met the Bruins in the conference finals. The Pens fell behind in the series, two games to none. Then they won four straight to reach the Stanley Cup Finals against the Minnesota North Stars.

The Penguins and North Stars traded wins in the first four games. But the Penguins then caught fire, notching 14 goals over the next six periods. After a 6-4 Pittsburgh victory in game five, the Penguins skated to an 8-0 rout in game six. Lemieux had scored 44 points in 23 postseason games to earn the Conn Smythe Trophy as playoff MVP. Pittsburgh had its first Stanley Cup after more than two decades of failures.

FACT:

JAROMIR JAGR WAS JUST A ROOKIE WHEN HIS PENS WON THE CUP IN 1991. HE WAS STILL PLAYING IN THE NHL IN 2017. BY THEN, HE WAS WITH HIS EIGHTH NHL TEAM AND HELD THE LEAGUE RECORD FOR GAME-WINNING GOALS.

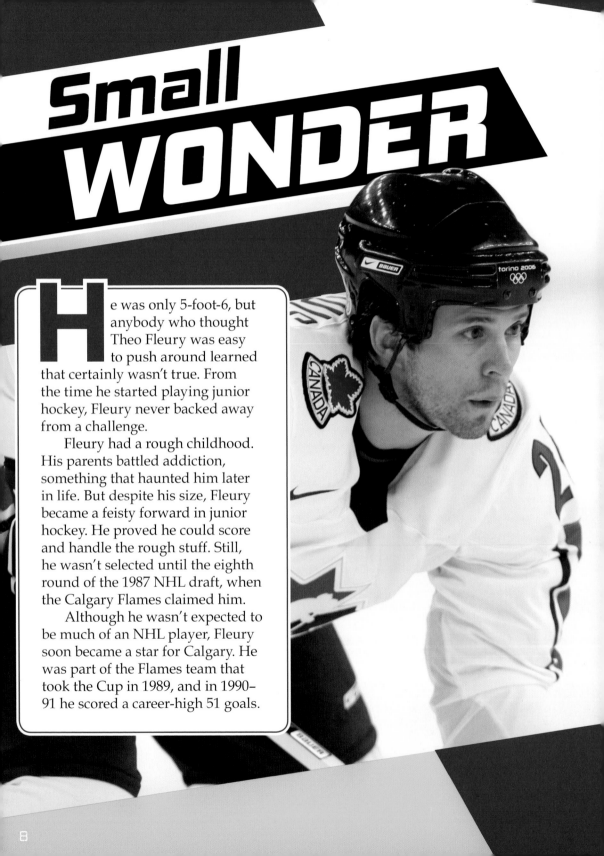

Small WONDER

He was only 5-foot-6, but anybody who thought Theo Fleury was easy to push around learned that certainly wasn't true. From the time he started playing junior hockey, Fleury never backed away from a challenge.

Fleury had a rough childhood. His parents battled addiction, something that haunted him later in life. But despite his size, Fleury became a feisty forward in junior hockey. He proved he could score and handle the rough stuff. Still, he wasn't selected until the eighth round of the 1987 NHL draft, when the Calgary Flames claimed him.

Although he wasn't expected to be much of an NHL player, Fleury soon became a star for Calgary. He was part of the Flames team that took the Cup in 1989, and in 1990–91 he scored a career-high 51 goals.

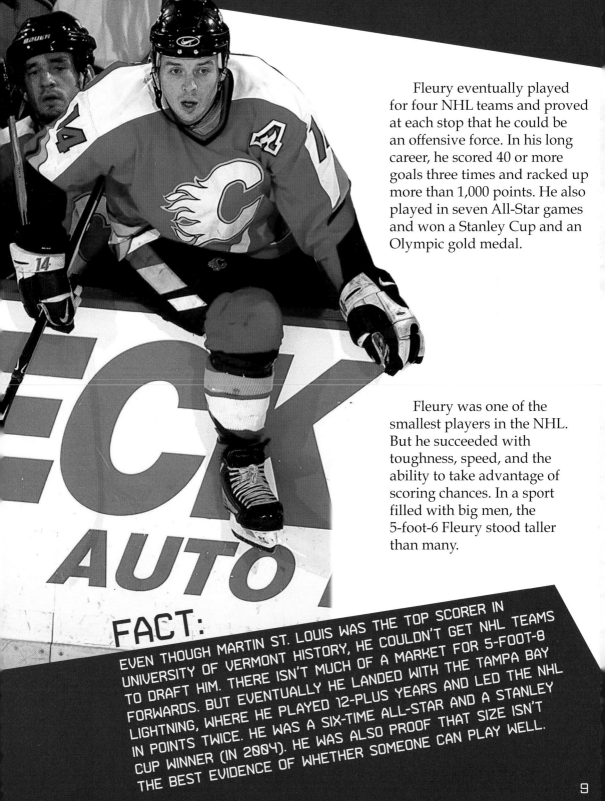

Fleury eventually played for four NHL teams and proved at each stop that he could be an offensive force. In his long career, he scored 40 or more goals three times and racked up more than 1,000 points. He also played in seven All-Star games and won a Stanley Cup and an Olympic gold medal.

Fleury was one of the smallest players in the NHL. But he succeeded with toughness, speed, and the ability to take advantage of scoring chances. In a sport filled with big men, the 5-foot-6 Fleury stood taller than many.

FACT:
EVEN THOUGH MARTIN ST. LOUIS WAS THE TOP SCORER IN UNIVERSITY OF VERMONT HISTORY, HE COULDN'T GET NHL TEAMS TO DRAFT HIM. THERE ISN'T MUCH OF A MARKET FOR 5-FOOT-8 FORWARDS. BUT EVENTUALLY HE LANDED WITH THE TAMPA BAY LIGHTNING, WHERE HE PLAYED 12-PLUS YEARS AND LED THE NHL IN POINTS TWICE. HE WAS A SIX-TIME ALL-STAR AND A STANLEY CUP WINNER (IN 2004). HE WAS ALSO PROOF THAT SIZE ISN'T THE BEST EVIDENCE OF WHETHER SOMEONE CAN PLAY WELL.

Toronto TRIPLE

The 1948–49 Toronto Maple Leafs were the two-time defending Stanley Cup champions, but they were underdogs. Never before had the reigning champs been held in such low regard. That year the Leafs had lost star forward and team captain Syl Apps. His absence showed during the regular season. The team finished 22–25–13, good for just fourth in the six-team NHL. Surely, they would not go far in the postseason.

Wrong. Behind 34-year-old Turk Broda, the most durable goalie in the league, the Leafs got hot at the right time. In the first round of the playoffs, Toronto stunned the Boston Bruins in five games. The Leafs had three goals in each of their wins. Max Bentley and Sid Smith handled much of the scoring, while Ted Kennedy's passing set them up. It was a great series win, but few people gave the Leafs much of a chance in the finals.

FACT:

THROUGH 2016, THE MAPLE LEAFS HAD THE NHL'S LONGEST CHAMPIONSHIP DROUGHT. ONCE A POWERHOUSE, THE LEAFS LAST WERE CHAMPS IN 1967. FORTY-EIGHT SEASONS HAVE PASSED.

They faced the Detroit Red Wings, a team that had finished with 18 more points than Toronto in the regular season. The Red Wings were led by stars Gordie Howe, Ted Lindsay, and Sid Abel. All three were budding legends whose numbers would someday be retired by their team.

Once again the Leafs had a big surprise for their opponents. Toronto won the first game in overtime, 3-2, and the next three by identical 3-1 scores. Between the pipes, Broda was excellent. He posted a goals-against average of 1.57 for the series. The Maple Leafs swept the Red Wings to take the Cup.

TORONTO WAS NOT ONLY THE FIRST TEAM TO WIN THREE CUPS IN A ROW, IT HAD ALSO SHOWN THE STRENGTH OF A CHAMPION'S HEART.

The BULLIES

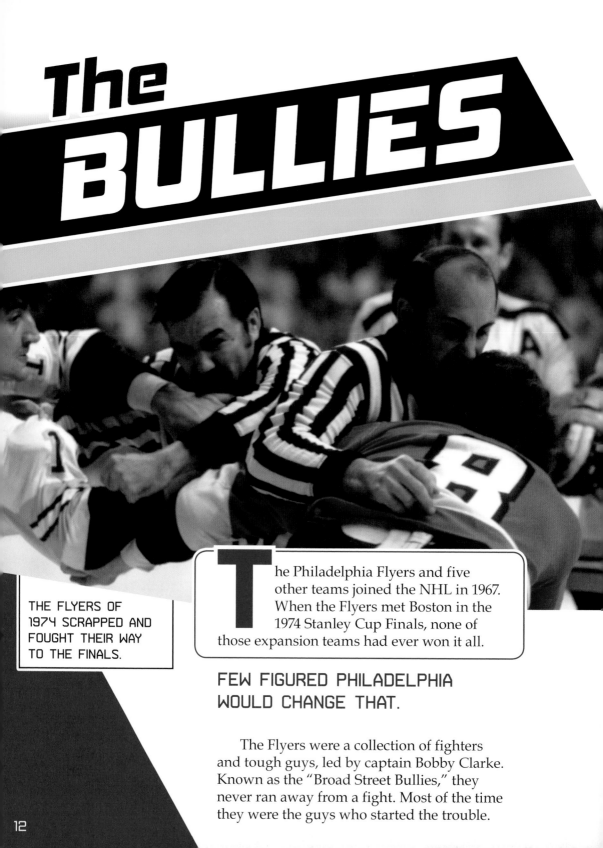

THE FLYERS OF
1974 SCRAPPED AND
FOUGHT THEIR WAY
TO THE FINALS.

The Philadelphia Flyers and five other teams joined the NHL in 1967. When the Flyers met Boston in the 1974 Stanley Cup Finals, none of those expansion teams had ever won it all.

FEW FIGURED PHILADELPHIA WOULD CHANGE THAT.

The Flyers were a collection of fighters and tough guys, led by captain Bobby Clarke. Known as the "Broad Street Bullies," they never ran away from a fight. Most of the time they were the guys who started the trouble.

The Bruins, meanwhile, were filled with established stars, including defenseman Bobby Orr, center Phil Esposito, and winger Ken Hodge. The Bruins had earned the most points in the NHL and scored the most goals. Winning it all wasn't supposed to be easy, but Boston felt confident. No member of the NHL's "Original Six" teams had lost to an expansion team in the finals.

The Bruins felt even better after winning the first game, 3-2. But the Flyers rebounded with an overtime win in the second game, beating Boston on its home rink. Philadelphia then won a pair of games at home to take a 3–1 advantage. In the sixth contest, outstanding Flyers goalie Bernie Parent shut down the Bruins. The Flyers' Rick MacLeish scored the only goal in a 1-0 victory. The Cup went to Philly, proving that the tough guys were just as good as anyone else.

BOBBY CLARKE CAPTAINED THE FLYERS AND NETTED A GAME-WINNING GOAL IN GAME 2, ONE OF HIS FIVE POSTSEASON GOALS.

FACT:
THE SIX TEAMS THAT JOINED THE NHL IN 1967 WERE THE LOS ANGELES KINGS, MINNESOTA NORTH STARS, CALIFORNIA SEALS, PHILADELPHIA FLYERS, PITTSBURGH PENGUINS, AND ST. LOUIS BLUES.

Hurricane WARNING

By the time the 2005–06 season began, the Carolina Hurricanes had gone three years without reaching the playoffs. Thanks to the 2004–05 lockout, they hadn't even played a game in more than 18 months. It's no wonder fans didn't have high expectations.

Nobody would have thought a second-year player such as Eric Staal would score 45 goals, after notching only 11 in his rookie season. And who would have predicted backup goalie Cam Ward would come off the bench and become the MVP of the Stanley Cup playoffs? It was a strange, wonderful season that began with uncertainty and ended with magic.

THE HURRICANES FACED THE EDMONTON OILERS FOR THE STANLEY CUP IN 2006.

The Hurricanes won the NHL's Southeast Division and racked up the second most points in the Eastern Conference. They whipped the Montreal Canadiens in the first round of the playoffs, thanks to Ward, who replaced regular goalie Martin Gerber. Carolina needed only five games to defeat the New Jersey Devils in the next round. The Buffalo Sabres proved tougher. The Sabres pushed the Hurricanes to seven games in the conference finals, but Carolina took the last game, 4-2.

The Canes would have to survive another seven-game series in the Stanley Cup Finals. The Canes took an early 2-0 lead and then held off the Edmonton Oilers to claim the Cup. The win was North Carolina's first professional sports championship and gave fans plenty to remember.

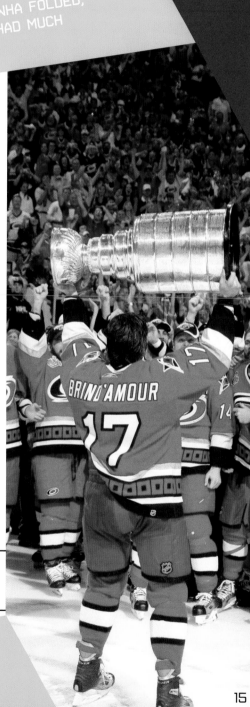

THE CANES AND THEIR FANS CELEBRATE THEIR FIRST CHAMPIONSHIP.

Rally of RALLIES

The Philadelphia Flyers had fallen into a 3–0 hole in their 2010 Eastern Conference semifinal against the Boston Bruins. The end of the Flyers' season looked to be coming quite soon. Only two NHL teams had ever overcome a three-game shortfall in a seven-game playoff series. Nobody had pulled off the feat in 35 years.

Few fans believed the Flyers could win the series. But instead of making plans for the summer, the Flyers stunned the hockey world with a remarkable comeback.

When Philadelphia won a 5-4 overtime decision in the fourth game, nobody in Boston's locker room was too concerned. Then Philly captured the next two games, 4-0 and 2-1, to set up a game seven showdown in Boston. One period into the game, it looked as if the Bruins would be just fine. They held a 3-0 lead, and fans were cranking up their celebration.

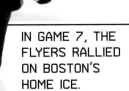

IN GAME 7, THE FLYERS RALLIED ON BOSTON'S HOME ICE.

The Flyers stormed back to tie the game. With nine minutes left, the Bruins were caught with too many men on the ice. The Flyers went on the power play, and Simon Gagne scored to give Philly a 4-3 advantage. That turned out to be the winning margin.

THE FLYERS HAD PULLED OFF A MIRACLE. AND BOSTON WAS LEFT TO WONDER HOW IT ALL HAPPENED.

THE FLYERS CELEBRATED WHILE THE BRUINS ABSORBED THE SHOCK OF THE LOSS.

FACT:

BEFORE THE FLYERS STUNNED THE BRUINS, ONLY TWO TEAMS HAD EVER REBOUNDED FROM A 3-0 DEFICIT IN THE POSTSEASON. IN 1942 THE MAPLE LEAFS CLIMBED OUT OF A THREE-GAME HOLE TO DEFEAT THE RED WINGS IN THE FINALS. THIRTY-THREE YEARS LATER, THE ISLANDERS SHOOK OFF A THREE-GAME DISADVANTAGE TO DUMP THE PENGUINS.

"It's really hard to find words for it," Bruins captain Zdeno Chara said after his team's defeat.

Philadelphia fans had no trouble doing that. They had lots of words for it. How about wonderful? Or remarkable? Amazing, astounding, and astonishing fit too.

"Our mindset was that if we were going to go down," Flyers captain Mike Richards said afterward, "we were going to go down swinging."

A Dynasty's
FIRST STEPS

Maybe it was the beards. When the New York Islanders entered the 1980 playoffs, some of their players decided not to shave. It's a pretty common practice now, but back then, it was something new.

Members of other teams laughed about it. But the Islanders were trying to make a statement that '80 would be different. They would let their whiskers grow until they claimed the Cup — or got eliminated from the playoffs.

THE ISLANDERS' STEFAN PERSSON, DENIS POTVIN, AND MIKE BOSSY (FROM LEFT) CELEBRATE AFTER A GOAL.

The Islanders had won their division the last two years, but they had suffered a pair of disappointing playoff losses. The Isles took second in the division in 1979–80, but they still had plenty of talent. Their stars included defenseman Denis Potvin, forward Bryan Trottier, and goalie Billy Smith. (All three of them would someday be inducted into the Hockey Hall of Fame.)

The Islanders ripped through the first two playoff rounds, beating the Los Angeles Kings and Boston Bruins. Many people began to believe this year would be different for New York. The Islanders reached the Stanley Cup Finals by beating the Buffalo Sabres in six games.

BEGINNING IN 1980, THE ISLANDERS HOISTED THE CUP FOUR YEARS IN A ROW.

They would face the Philadelphia Flyers, and that was no small challenge. The Flyers had earned the NHL's most points during the regular season and had finished well above New York in the division standings.

The Islanders won game one when Potvin scored in overtime. New York had a 3-1 advantage in games before the Flyers won the fifth game. When game six went to overtime, Bob Nystrom clinched the Isles' first-ever Stanley Cup by redirecting a pass from John Tonelli into the net.

And giving the Islanders an excuse to shave.

BILLY SMITH WAS A STAR NET-MINDER.

Delayed GLORY

For years Tim Thomas bounced around the Finnish, Swedish, and North American minor leagues, hoping for a shot at the big time. He couldn't have dreamed he would become one of the world's best goalies. He just wanted a chance. For parts of seven seasons, Thomas was away from the big time.

He wanted to play in the NHL, not in Europe and certainly not in the minors.

His big chance didn't come until 2002. Thomas was 28 years old when he signed with the Boston Bruins. His age and experience didn't mean he would start right away. That took another four seasons. By the 2008–09 campaign, Thomas had proved the wait was worth it. He took over as the Bruins' regular net-minder, played in the All-Star game, and won the Vezina Trophy as the NHL's best goalie.

TIM THOMAS

Two years later Thomas was even better. He won the Vezina again, shut out nine teams, and was the MVP of the Stanley Cup playoffs. He also led the Bruins to their first Stanley Cup title in 39 years. Thomas allowed only 1.98 goals a game during the playoffs. Not bad for a guy who almost didn't make it.

IN 2011 THOMAS SET A RECORD FOR SAVES IN A SINGLE POSTSEASON WITH WITH 798.

FACT:

SOME PRO HOCKEY PLAYERS SPEND TIME IN THE MINORS BEFORE REACHING AN NHL CLUB. OTHER PLAYERS SPEND THEIR ENTIRE CAREERS THERE. THE NHL HAS TIES TO TWO LEAGUES WHERE IT DEVELOPS PROSPECTS. THEY ARE THE AMERICAN HOCKEY LEAGUE AND THE EAST COAST HOCKEY LEAGUE. A THIRD CIRCUIT, THE INTERNATIONAL HOCKEY LEAGUE, SURVIVED FROM 1945 TO 2001. WHEN IT FOLDED, SIX OF THE SEVEN IHL MEMBERS JOINED THE AHL.

Out of NOWHERE

Pavel Datsyuk was certainly not going to cry after he was passed over twice in the NHL draft. He had known real tragedy. He had lost his mother when he was still a teenager. Instead the young Russian kept on working, hoping that someday he would get a shot. Finally the Detroit Red Wings chose him at the end of the sixth round in 1998. Datsyuk, who had first excelled at soccer, was on his way to big things on the ice.

Datsyuk needed time to get comfortable in Detroit, even though the Wings had several other Russian players on the roster. Once he settled in, Datsyuk became one of the league's top defensive forwards. Three times he won the league's award in that category, called the Frank J. Selke Trophy. Datsyuk was also a four-time recipient of the Lady Byng Trophy, which goes to the player who exhibits the best sportsmanship.

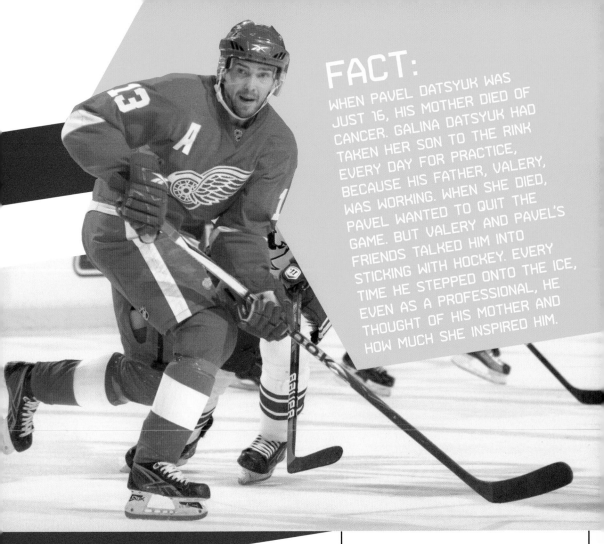

PAVEL DATSYUK PLAYED IN 157 POSTSEASON GAMES FOR THE WINGS, NETTING 42 GOALS.

Datsyuk was named to four All-Star teams and played on a pair of Detroit Stanley Cup winners, in 2002 and 2008. He scored 30 or more goals in three seasons and registered 97 points in 2007–08 and 2008–09. Datsyuk spent his 14-year career with Detroit as one of the league's most consistent forwards. He left the NHL to play in his native Russia after the 2015–16 season.

DATSYUK'S CAREER ALSO SERVED AS A LESSON TO ALL NHL TEAMS TO BE MORE CAREFUL WHEN EVALUATING PLAYERS.

Devil of a SEASON

I t was all supposed to happen during the 1993–94 season. The New Jersey Devils were supposed to win the Cup. They had posted 106 points, the most in franchise history. But they couldn't defeat their bitter rivals, the New York Rangers, in the playoffs. The Devils fell in a classic conference finals series that went seven games.

THE DEVILS WON THE STANLEY CUP THREE TIMES WITH MARTIN BRODEUR BETWEEN THE PIPES.

FACT:

WHEN THE ROLL OF THE GREATEST GOALIES IN NHL HISTORY IS CALLED, MARTIN BRODEUR IS ALWAYS NEAR THE TOP. THE NINE-TIME ALL-STAR WON THREE STANLEY CUPS AND TWO OLYMPIC GOLD MEDALS. HE HOLDS THE NHL RECORD FOR MOST REGULAR SEASON WINS (691) AND SHUTOUTS (125). BRODEUR WON THE VEZINA TROPHY AS THE LEAGUE'S BEST GOALTENDER FOUR TIMES.

The Devils weren't overpowering in the 1994–95 regular season, but once the playoffs started, Jersey came together. With captain Scott Stevens and outstanding goaltender Martin Brodeur leading the way, New Jersey lost only four games in three series wins. After the huge disappointment the year before, the Devils had reached the Stanley Cup Finals.

Waiting for them were the Detroit Red Wings. The Wings had won the Presidents' Trophy for earning the most points during the regular season. Detroit was the heavy favorite, having lost only two playoff games on the way to the finals.

But the Devils stunned Detroit. They took the first two games in the Motor City to set an NHL record with 10 road playoff wins. Back in New Jersey, the Devils scored a pair of 5-2 victories to sweep the series. The Devils raised the Cup and erased the bad memories from a year earlier.

Unlikely All-Star HERO

The criticism was relentless. John Scott simply didn't belong in the 2016 NHL All-Star game. He had scored a total of five goals during his entire career and was known more for his fighting than his offensive skills. He stood 6-foot-8 and weighed 260 pounds — not exactly a typical hockey All-Star. But the fans wanted him there, and they voted him onto the team.

JOHN SCOTT PLAYED FOR SEVEN NHL TEAMS FROM 2008 TO 2016.

IN FACT, SO MANY PEOPLE VOTED FOR SCOTT THAT HE WAS NAMED CAPTAIN OF THE PACIFIC DIVISION TEAM.

Scott had bounced between the minors and the NHL for years, but fans started an effort to make him an All-Star. They spread the word via social media, generating more interest. Scott received enough votes to be Pacific Division captain, even though he was in the minors.

Some media members were upset by the move. They said it made the game a joke. Scott didn't care. He was happy to be playing. And even though he had never been much of an offensive threat, Scott scored two goals to lead his team to victory. Many fans loved it.

When it came time to vote for the MVP, Scott was again a big winner, thanks to a Twitter campaign that secured the honor. It was the perfect way to end a remarkable weekend. Lots of fans said it proved that Scott belonged there after all.

The next year the NHL said no player who was in the minors could be a captain, no matter how many votes he received. Scott, who had retired after the 2015–16 season, was okay with that. After all, he already had his big moment.

SCOTT MADE THE MOST OF HIS ALL-STAR MOMENT.

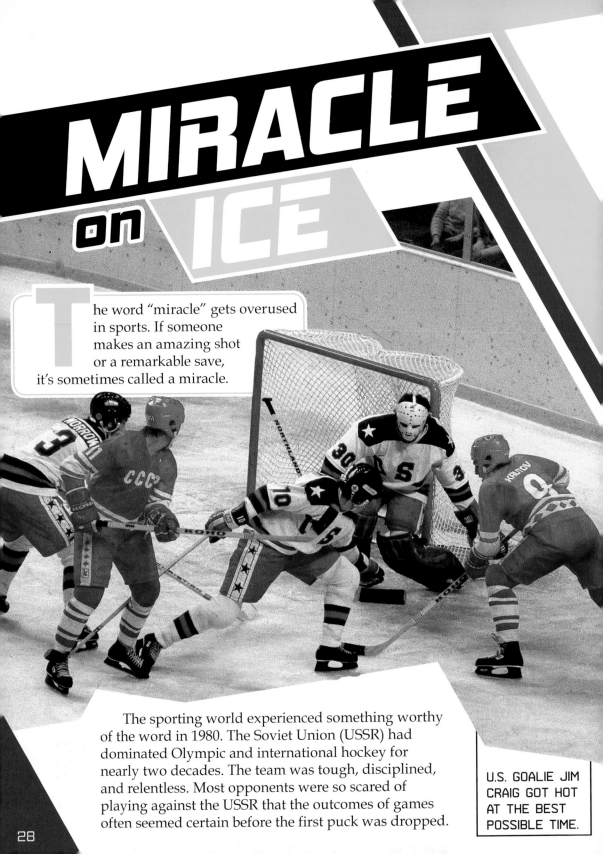

MIRACLE on ICE

The word "miracle" gets overused in sports. If someone makes an amazing shot or a remarkable save, it's sometimes called a miracle.

The sporting world experienced something worthy of the word in 1980. The Soviet Union (USSR) had dominated Olympic and international hockey for nearly two decades. The team was tough, disciplined, and relentless. Most opponents were so scared of playing against the USSR that the outcomes of games often seemed certain before the first puck was dropped.

U.S. GOALIE JIM CRAIG GOT HOT AT THE BEST POSSIBLE TIME.

The U.S. Olympic team hadn't beaten the Soviets in Olympic play since 1960. The Americans were considered a major underdog going into the 1980 Games. A big reason was the 10-3 beating the Soviets gave Team USA two weeks before the Olympics began.

Maybe the Soviets were overconfident when they met the U.S. team in the Olympic Games at Lake Placid, New York. Perhaps the Americans had overcome their fear of the mighty USSR team. When the teams faced off in the medal round, it was a much different game.

The game stood tied, 2-2, after the first period, a surprising result. After two periods the score was 3-2, with the USSR ahead. But third-period goals by Mark Johnson and captain Mike Eruzione gave the Americans a 4-3 lead that they didn't give up.

Just before the final siren sounded, ABC TV's Al Michaels cried, "Do you believe in miracles? Yes!" An entire nation was with him.

TEAM USA CELEBRATES ITS STUNNING WIN.

FACT:
IT WOULD HAVE BEEN HARD TO FIND A PLAYER ON THE U.S. HOCKEY TEAM WHO HAD MUCH LOVE FOR HEAD COACH HERB BROOKS. THE MINNESOTA NATIVE WAS TOUGH AND DIDN'T ALWAYS TREAT THE PLAYERS VERY WELL. BUT HE HAD A PLAN. BROOKS MADE THE AMERICANS PRACTICE HARD, AND HE CRITICIZED ANYBODY WHO RELAXED. HE MADE THE U.S. TEAM BELIEVE THAT IT COULD BEAT THE WORLD'S BEST.

Underdog
ROUNDUP

Chris Kunitz: Even though Kunitz had a big senior season at Ferris State University, no NHL team thought enough of his talent to draft him. Eventually, the Anaheim Ducks signed him, but it took two years for Kunitz to become a full-time player. Now with the Pittsburgh Penguins, he is a reliable winger who has scored 20 or more goals seven times, including 35 in 2013–14.

Steve Thomas: When Thomas was in school, a teacher once told him, "Smarten up, Steve. Hockey can only take you so far." Thomas tried harder in his studies, but he didn't stop playing hockey, which ended up giving him quite a ride. Even though he went undrafted, Thomas started his NHL career with the Toronto Maple Leafs in 1984 and ended it 20 years later after time spent with five other clubs. Thomas scored 30 or more goals five times and topped 40 twice.

Tyler Bozak: Maybe it was because of his injured knee that Bozak went undrafted in 2009. But the Toronto Maple Leafs were smart enough to sign him to a contract. Though it took a season for him to become a full-time contributor, Bozak remains a strong presence at forward for the Leafs and scored 23 goals in 2014–15.

Dan Girardi: According to the scouts, Girardi wasn't skilled enough to play in the NHL. But Girardi believed in himself and bugged NHL teams to give him a tryout. The New York Rangers agreed to look at him and signed him to a contract. After spending parts of three seasons in the minors, Girardi got his shot with the big club in 2006. Once he got on the ice, he rarely left, missing only 13 games in nine seasons and becoming an alternate captain.

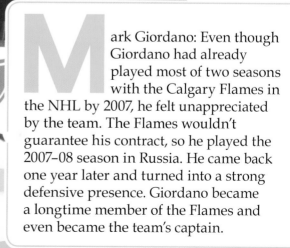

Mark Giordano: Even though Giordano had already played most of two seasons with the Calgary Flames in the NHL by 2007, he felt unappreciated by the team. The Flames wouldn't guarantee his contract, so he played the 2007–08 season in Russia. He came back one year later and turned into a strong defensive presence. Giordano became a longtime member of the Flames and even became the team's captain.

READ MORE

Editors of Sports Illustrated Kids. *Face-Off: Top Ten Lists of Everything in Hockey.* New York: Sports Illustrated, 2015.

Frederick, Shane. *Hockey's Record Breakers.* North Mankato, Minn.: Capstone Press, 2017.

Hawkins, Jeff. *Playing Pro Hockey.* Minneapolis: Lerner Publications, 2014.

INTERNET SITES

Use FactHound to find Internet sites related to this book.

Visit www.facthound.com

Just type in 9781515780458 and go.

INDEX